JAZZ TALMUD

Designed and typeset by The Sheep Meadow Press.
Distributed by The University Press of New England.

All inquiries and permission requests should be addressed to the publisher:

The Sheep Meadow Press
P.O. Box 84
Rhinebeck, NY 12572

Library of Congress Cataloging-in-Publication Data

Marmer, Jake.
Jazz Talmud / Jake Marmer.
    p. cm.
Poems.
ISBN 978-1-931357-88-3
I. Title.
PS3613.A76664J39 2011
811'.6--dc22

                                    2011026805

Poems in this collection have previously appeared in *The Drunken Boat*, the *Forward, Blue Jew Yorker, Flying Fish, Mima'amakim Journal of Jewish Art, New Vilna Review,* and Mediterranean.nu. "Tel Aviv Vignette" was chosen as the winner of the London School of Jewish Studies Poetry Competition in 2010 and featured in the LSJS newsletter.

JAZZ TALMUD

POEMS

JAKE MARMER

THE SHEEP MEADOW PRESS
RHINEBECK, NEW YORK

First of all fruits, to Jerusalem
To Shana & Lev,
My Jerusalem

TABLE OF CONTENTS

1

2

1

Mishnah Cycle

Mishnah of Visions

Rav Iver was born blind,
but got around having exquisitely
sharpened his sense of smell.
He could not only recognize people
and bouquets of their moods,
but also world's faintest abstractions.
Truth, he said, smells like bleach.
Lies? Like truth. Existential crisis—
drop of tender buckwheat honey
in a barrel of Russian tea.
He also said: as I am
in front of you today, soul
is a blind man facing a mirror.
I say soul's a blind man
knocking on the mirror.
He was reborn roughly
two thousand years later
as Blind Lemon Jefferson
but instead of inhaling the visions
this time around
he heard them, and
they were blue—
blue, blue, blue.

JAZZ TALMUD

said Rabbi Zusha: "my mother named me Sasha but I fell into a seraphic orchestra pit, and things have not been the same"   his students asked him: "what did you see in the pit?"   he answered: "behold: four seraphs held a cello, like a naked, newly-formed body, and eight pushed the bow" whose cello? Adam's   whose bow? Mordechai's   the refused bow that makes cellos of heaven sing the soul-spilling human heaviness—the essence   he also said: "in every horn, there lives a family of shadadademons—a family of three or four—on the average   angel Gabriel comes to blow his hot breath to let them loose into the world, their clothes flutter, their hearts beat against the four brass bars of domestication, both breaking as a result"   therefore, every saxophone is a ripped cage: no, a rib cage: rib cage of an ancient being that de-composed long before names of god became the star-tallis in which hearts are wrapped/rapt   taught Rabbi Akiva: behold there are names of god that got filtered by moth-screens   others got lost in the loss of the hiss of the vinyl   some stuck in Karl Marx's beard   some stuck between the boards of the family-table and can only be extracted with a big family knife   some spilled on the mama-apron in the deep-fry-metaphysical back-kitchen   but these are the 32 revealed names of god: "jehwaep. shadai-doodah woop helohadip dip papadoo dap. strata doo dampa flip clip dedam pam pa peanuts dereederedere salt strip tzuris degatee goat boom dupa goat ratata ratata what? you askin? outer bank, jehwaep shadai doodah wap"   New Orleans funk band the Meters inherited twelve crumbs of the god-name from the loa grandma who plucked them at the foot of the great phal-lic Ethiopian Eucalyptus   but some say she birthed these crumbs, each in deep pain, each deep in time, each under the brilliant lamp-lights, which are the eyes of Messiah himself.

THE LAWS OF DREAM-COOKING

"There's no cooking after cooking:" once a dream has been in the oven for two thousand years, it's done and nothing that happens to it is considered cooking. That's if a dream is a solid. If a liquid, it may have long evaporated and you're deluding yourself over an empty burning pot. But, if the dream is a sound, an invisible musical cloud, then you are the one being cooked: on the endless spinning vinyl, zapped into music by needles of history.

—*After Babylonian Talmud, Shabbat 145B*

BATHHOUSE OF DREAMS

In Aphrodite's bathhouse in Akko, Proklos ben
Plosphos asked Rav Gamliel: "So rabbi, what are
you here to wash?" "My umm . . . my umbilical,"
answered Gamliel. "Every morning I find a new
hole in my blanket-edges burnt with acidic dream-
sweat, dream-sweat of the great Void. Every
morning my ears are full of afterbirth, my hands are
covered with yellow slime. If not for your
Aphrodite's foam, if not for all of your wine-
shadows and soul geometry, I'd stay a perpetual
new dream-born, a locked suitcase . . .

DREAMEMORY

dreamemory: stumbled
real or echo stuck
between teeth
between morning
mountains
Ebal and Gerizim?
Some say: dreamemory
is dust
leftover from Adam's making.
Some say no:
regular
window dust.
Others say: gravel.
The gravel?
     The gravel.
     In Beit El—
     Jacob's rockpile dream—
     our crushed nomad pillow
         all of these are the living   *eilu veilu veilu*
     words of the living god   *divrei elohim chayim*

BEBOP HISTORY OF THE EXILE

popped string: we
melody-unzipped we know
a thing or two about
we know   nah—
thing we know
about the tube: the birth: the pre:
this thing of nah-thing, thing of
boundless we:
we boundless
we nothing boundless
we're bound
bound-up!
down in the rotten Russian bathtub, down the ice
the ice of we, and the pitch
black pitch we know
nothing, the silence—
but nothing is silent about the pitch!
Yael pitching skies
over Sisera's sleep
he sunk he fell he lay
between her skies between her thighs
and the rhythm was all in her
she went uh-one-TWO-three-four, laying back, one-TWO-three-four
she sang one chorus
but her shadows kept banging
over and over as if into winter
earth that won't give, as if into god-behind-the-ice—
the god of nowhere
to go but inward, call it nah—
thing, the song
of someone pulling
our big exilic bathtub
with a popped string, we
melody-unzipped we

MISHNAH OF LONELINESS

There're three types of loneliness in the world: green, red,
and purple. So says the house of Hillel. In the house of
Shammai, they say: loneliness
is either black or white; all other types
don't exist and require a sacrifice of a young goat:
your internal goat.

Says Rava: in all of my years, I have not known loneliness.
All day I'm at the yeshiva with you nudniks, then I come
home to groveling domestic tractates. One day, I stepped
outside and screamed: Master, I want you in silence, in
absence, in wordless music of our solitude! Right then I
saw a great ladder, reaching to the Throne up high. The
Throne—was empty—but up and down the steps, there
went lost sounds, scales of unused and discarded words,
slip-ups, swallowed hallucinations, choked on ecstasies—a
whole decontextualized orchestra racing like goats through
the fog. The voice said: this, Rava, is the room of my
absence, music of our solitude. You like it? Go home! Stuff
your ears with pages of sophistry, eat, make a bad pun for
that is the meaning of peace.

MISHNAH OF SILENCE

Said Rav Yehuda: even silence has its laws, even silence.

Even silence: smooth, perfectly pressed dry-cleaned trouser silence. But the odd-looking, wrinkled silence chewed up into a broken cosmic accordion is lawless, different every time.

Said Rav Ashi: kosher silence is always pregnant. But the other silence is simply having nothing to say—in the company of others—nothing at all, not even in jest, nothing about the weather, not a single word of thanks: How could you? Therefore, you should always talk, mumble if you must. Even if you don't speak the language of your mouth. Even if you're alone, even if your mouth broke—talk with your hands, eyes, genitals, but never stop talking.

Said Hillel: you must be silent three times a day. The improvised silence, drawn from your helpless inarticulate insides is also a prayer—to the abyss, communion with discoloration, mother of all misery: an anti-prayer prayer. You can only recite it when you're dead, and only with nine other dead Jewish males.

Jazz Golem

jazz golem scratched his couch-dust into life into late-night face of the dustpan street of the
kadabra living dusty Brooklyn dust!
he brought clarinet to his lips and the spirit of Dave Tarras blew life into him
jazz golem erased the four Hebrew letters off his forehead
and was still alive and breathing—as a regular assimilated Brooklyn golem
ready to live another two thousand years
jazz golem screamed out the whole Talmud, Jerusalem to Babylon
so fast so fast it blurred all letters all laws into a single musical string
blew Talmudic shapes into bubbling maddening speedy shapes
of pure music a jazz groan across the rhythms of uneasy Brooklyn sleep
he outraced god he didn't
believe in and was alone still screaming the infinite
Talmud and his every chorus was what
if there's more, what
if there's more
of what? he flew higher than any note Elijah ever blown
and punched the—empty—sky till it was black and blue
with intimations of sunrise

Mishnah Number Name

There's no 3 after 4 unless 6 and 25. Every morning you should 75, and in the afternoons with others, 112. The dog is 5. Dog in heat, 4. Doorpost: 3; I know 3. Now, 614: picket fence; also Isaac's knife; television, and the camera—for camera's sake. Said Rabbi Yehuda: god is 8—glasses turned upside, plastic infinity holding the lens, and as for us—all decimals, all behind a 0.

LOOPHOLE

With thanks to D.O.

If you must move
that which can't be touched
move it,
touching it
in a way no one would ever think
of touching it.
Being something that doesn't happen
it won't happen.
There won't be a word to describe what you're doing:
you can get as close as you like.
Not even our untouchable
God will realize
moving near you
like a gullible bird
moving straight
into your Talmudic glove,
set at the gaping mouth of the loophole.

TOHU (VACUUM)

If Rabbi Nachman was born today
(now that we understand god
doesn't exist)
he wouldn't be teaching Torah
wouldn't be running his starved flesh
through the infinite hermeneutic labyrinths
he'd work for Disney
maybe, the General Motives
come home and read
alone, all night

and the drop

between these two worlds
would be big enough, even for Rabbi Nachman

MISHNAH OF AESTHETICS

Students asked Rabbi Akiva: "What is beauty?" The
master immediately turned into a human-sized carp.
It was a hot Babylonian summer. His distinguished
lips opened with a silent plea and students rushed
him into the nearest ritual bath, a *mikvah*, where he
regained composure and replied: "I don't know
what beauty is, but in this heat, it can surely kill
you!"

UMTZA
Passover Freedom Free-Jazz Solo

Said Rabbi Meir: "Any time Torah says "matza" it really means "umtza" What is um-
tza?   I don't know, you tell me   Yeah, umtza is umtza-talking   What? No such word
exists.   Umtza-scatting is umtza-scattering. And crumbling.   What?? What is this
umtza matza?   I tell you it's no umtza-*matza* It's umtza-umtza   Which is?   About
keeping it dry, the climate inside of you, keeping it a desert, umtza-umtza. Children of
Israel carried freedom on their backs, umtza-umtza. Pyramid of freedom, camel-shit,
Egyptian loot, umtza-umtza. Riding them like a snare. Can you feel it? Whole Nile a
mirror of their own Mississippi faces! Eagle faces, with lion behinds! Had there ever
been another way? Umtza-umtza freedom drang, Torah allegro non-troppo all through
the desert, primal-tribal umtza-umtza, not by bread alone but by the unseizable umtza
umtza dubbah dum is that the manna they collected? And how they baked it on their
backs, coulda tasted any way they wanted but somehow every time they turned it into
umtza umtza umtzaumtza for breakfast umtzaumtzaumtzalunch and if they found wa-
ter they'd really just slow it down like a victorious little reggae-style march umtzatza
umtzatza   umtzatza And since then, seven days a year, don't be eating nothing but
your own dry obsession, nervous fingers banging, as you're crouching, by the umtza
table nervous fingers massaging the lips stiff from all that sitting down these lips been
sitting in the same umtza-song-position a little too long is this a virus, a soul-virus?   It's
the law, umtza-umtza. You can never stop, or the umtza race will be over! Who's gonna
sing when you gone, umtza-umtza, in this unredeemed hungry world, we'd be off the
ground in no time, without the umtza-umtza. It's your shovel to dig yourself a home,
umtza-home. Dig under the Passover table, let your children and their children's chil-
dren, even four generations, all at the same time, all together umtza-umtza, no Bbbb
ba-buh ba-brread not even bababa beboppapababaeans, only . . .

WEEKDAY ANGEL

Angel Gabriel had a fear of heights
and so stayed down, hunched on
two flimsy angelic legs, neck shivering,
terrified forehead, gaze below the horizon—

had he not been invisible
he'd be shoved in a puddle by morning subway rush
had his eyes not been made of Hebrew letters
they'd be tearing in New York winter wind
had his soul not been made of fire
        he'd be melted by the red sun
                setting over Manhattan an hour
                        before the workday's end.

THE LAW

Halakha—the Law—is the wheelchair of God
God's fiery wheelchair chariot
horizontal dreams of transcendence
Jacob's ladder turned into a railroad track.

Midrash as Gossip

calmly, Talmudic breath blowing
over morning coffee
as if God's over the Red Sea,
he repeats word for word things Leah
said to Jacob first time they had breakfast together
ah, Jacob—he never forgave himself
for his father's weakness
neither with Leah nor Rachel,
could never go up *that* ladder, until—

the week before the holiday of Shavuot
Ruth is on his tabloids, as he flashes
hermeneutic shots of her laying
at the feet of Boaz: she, hyper-aware
of her, you could say, passport, but with enough
desire and beauty to bend the rod
of the law—

and her descendent, King David?
Whose eyes wrote a psalm on the tiles
around Batsheva's bathtub?
When it's patriarchs, it's not adultery:
it's glamour—*clamor*-glamour, before
the Almighty: someone had to do it,
and now we can rest, peacefully, on
the carpeted archives of rabbinic commentary

don't get me wrong: he spoke for the sake of
heaven—but when one day he was heard saying
did you hear the one about . . . the one . . .
the one about—the one? the One??—
doubting, short-circuiting, in a sudden self-reading slippage
he blanked out and found himself

covered in snow
Miriam's snowy
leprosy—
and for seven days sat alone, without a coat or a hat,
thinking all things *she* might have been
whispering about

PROGRESS

in this 21st century
when angel Gabriel sings
it is no longer to break
the big cold stone
stuck in God's heart
the stone
must now pass
through the bladder
of an even bigger and greater God
the one we
don't actually believe in.

GOD

god is a tongue
a conveyer belt
purveyor of superb
nonsense shaped like a tongue
a carpet of taste buds
each, a word tasting
vacuum in its own way
(in its own *vey*)
sorry if the image
isn't very worship-conducive
but it is
in the image of—
us all
in the image of—
we're all in this
       together
       warped
       universe-wide photograph
touched up every second
and by everybody

THELONIOUS MONK IN JERUSALEM

the window broke so many
times and sun's autograph
on the window burns
big lips of Jerusalem
gods, kissing the outside
slurring summer gods
      of the crumpled
sweaty note-sheets
gods of the off: the window broke so many
times one hung-over
        cloud-lip

    hanging

hermeneutic owl
spectacles are watching
    our Batsheva's footsteps
drying up on the royal floor
hey what's the deal with this obsession
    over a few footsteps
on the cracked royal floor

      (cracked per cracking
    of the proverbial jugs
      of Isaac Luria)

          under a thin blanket
       thin thin blanket
     Jerusalem, barely morning

Monk's directive over the headphones:

dream-sift through

the night's fill of Jerusalem

        trying on Monk's gloves my fingers

       stretch out to city's every piano
rib-cage piano, piano-piano
fingers tapping the hot
Jerusalem windows
glass burning like our backs, graffiti of sunburn, Monk's game

of avoiding
disaster by a hair, sweaty
hair sweaty
for weeks through this long Mediterranean summer

FOREFATHER INTO
(Sketches over Zohar)

who'd think going
        would involve this much sitting

    two a.m. desert refugee fugue-bop sessions
    with our five big mouths sticking out of the sand, breathing in
    through the horns, crooked breaths punctuating the eighths,
    our bodies, communally petrified, waiting to rise but in the meantime

so much potential vomit, vomit inside,
every song is soaked in it

everything that corresponded perfectly
        broke down here, at the edge of the center of the world

        Haran

  where I begun selling the off-balance as holiness door-to-door

            two weeks out,
           rain over steel
          drum, Shkhinah's melodious patterns of rejection

    my parents are dead to me

        when the sandal got slammed in the door, couldn't deal
        and now I just don't have doors

           the wife's too beautiful for comfort

sky says: you are the definition of love,
    the world didn't know what love was until you came around

now   un-bury the creation, let it eat   your shovel

Shkhinah (Hebrew): Divine presence.

33

DA LIFNEI MI: IMPROVISATION ON THE THEME

"Da Lifnei Mi Atah Omed," Hebrew for "Know In Front of Whom You Stand" is
traditionally written atop of the ark in synagogues.

da lifney mi atah
omed: eyes closed whose head
are you dreaming into
whose head are you in?

to da lifney maaaah—mamamah—mama? mi-? Miles? Moma—Modern Art Museum in New
York?
i gotta get this down for sure, who you

who you in front of—

but how could you even . . . ? No!
no-in-G, flat G, on the alto sax
same as F-sharp: for the left hand, all yr fingers will be down, and you can do anything you
want
with your right

da dadada dududu dada dududu dudada
lifnei mi lifnei ma

know-in-G, flat knowin-g
the ultimate flatness of the ancient matza-desert-earth-parchment
and then, the beef tongue mountain:
and we're pores, we're nerve-endings,
yes us nEErve endings of the beef tongue of the almighty

in front of who we

whose face are we

whose face-lift lifnei our own,   who gives the quickest NO?

—honey, who've you been—fighting with? there're
fingerprints all over yr glasses
you should wash them
—these are no fingerprints but the patriarchal angelic self-
grabbing impulses to grab the desire touch the eyeballs the
ears touch the moment of
reception of the moment of desire
I want

to da lifnei mi
lifnei do-re-mi

da/net da/net da/net

da lifney ma
da-fort-da

(da-fort-da was related to the child's great cultural achievement—the instinctual renunciation)
(that is, the renunciation of instinctual satisfaction) which he had made in allowing his mother to
go away without protesting)

lifnei mama lifnei mimo
                    [in Russian, mimo means off-target, mimammo is the off-mama, the
            father]
in front of who you

who? where?

where? in Potiphar's house: if reflection in the window
was NOT fatherly let-down of grey-haired limpid righteousness
if only it wasn't if only you could da what kinda world would it be if you could da all over
Potiphar's house and in general anywhere anytime with anyone and u know many of us tried and
many got tired but most many got shot, yes shot! down! by the mi—sha-me me, the big who—
who you in front of—

35

GIVING BACK

when your tongue finally scrapes
the bottom of your belief system
revealing the plastic container that held it
don't just dump it
in the garbage
gently place it into the blue
recycling bin
the planet and other people
still need it

ALTERNATIVE

wasn't loneliness
or hormones
I don't think it was
for a few years
something burned around me
a certainty, a need
even today I'm hopeful
as to where it came from
and I'd never defend ignorance
or insularism
but had my mind mushroomed
the other way
it wouldn't be the matter of blind bliss
or submissiveness
maybe the reality itself would appear different
thoughts linking not so
even these words
wouldn't stay in my pocket like pebbles
but fly upwards
or at least diagonally

2

VISA

Esther fasted three days before opening
the door of the King's room
praying that her unauthorized entry
be taken in stride.
That became Purim.

I once fasted through
a long summer day
before getting in line
at the American Embassy in Kiev
where I returned to renew my expired visa.

I thought about the Purim night
just half year prior, when
I was stopped
in the West Village
by undercover gents
for smoking a festive joint.

Getting in line at the embassy
(it forms at sunrise)
I laid *tefillin* asking
that the manila folder bearing my name
stay with the local
New York bureaucrats and
thankfully it did, though
what I burned through
inside, standing on that line,
I couldn't bring myself
to tell you, King.

But, King Ahasuerus,
I could tell you

about the afternoon
I spent at 27 Nablus Road
in East Jerusalem
at the American Consulate where
I needed to renew yet again
the only place in the universe
I've seen Jews and Arabs
praying in the same room—

above their heads
on synced television screens,
cartoons of matchstick people
signing papers and carrying suitcases, while
over them a slow, deliberate voice
telling everyone that lying
could lead to deportation and
how only a very, very small
percentage of applicants are granted entry.

FIRST THOUGHT

First thought:
redress-immigrant-thought thought
syntax migraine, loss-ellipses, then right away
sunglasses over those ellipses.
And so what you get
is a certain cooled
suspendered eloquence—
backwash fluidity, if you will.

GANELIN TRIO
Vision Festival 2007

bars/free jazz con-troll   free jazz limp   limb control free
like the bass-line not there but you know what it is—

out! golden teeth! not saxophone's but friendly, innocent but out
I don't (don't) want to hear anyone speaking Russian
unless it's inside a memory not even   burns into me shudders me
the me-shudders shutter-bang maybe sun through the magnifying glass? or sun in the mirror
MIRr   or

you know, I've actually changed seats on the subway, and in Central Park, and now here—
second time already   they
came out to see the trio of course, not the peeling pre-Soviet Jews of the Lower East Side long
gone but the—of course—knowing the pianist is named Slava and sax is Petras easy to explain
the flurry of darkness alto gone cough-beyond-coughing, a man-pipe hailed on, hailed hail Slava
hail

s-lava! free jazz-limb con-trol free jazz role-free

its a peeling shul, ex-shul, now a peeling arts center, and Russian pianist from Israel but his
drummer is German I wonder where they rehearse the two ruined walls inside of them who do I
hate more today self or the other but don't go there not there how wrong but they go isn't this
cough-beyond-coughing exactly that?   backs facing the wall-peel

we're all weightless and beautiful and mesmerizing
we're all weightless and beautiful and mesmerizing

                              (the finale a little too sudden for me—was time to
press the button and he just pressed it—)

DEALINGS

every few years when it snows really hard in New York
someone inevitably comments: this is nothing for you, right?
you people are used to much heavier stuff—
but the truth is that the provincial town I come from
in the steppes of Ukraine was not big on winter
in fact it never snowed: when the weather turned
and clouds got heavy, what fell from the skies was not snow but playing cards
of very small denominations, cards meant for losing,
that some angry Slavic god emptied out on his people
as they landed on men's shoulder's like epaulettes of ignobility
if you want to know, it wasn't very different
from what goes down in your Atlantic city, not altogether unlike
midtown streets littered with the same bad cards, one of which
I've just turned over, for your reading pleasure.

THE BIG MOMENT

landed on his shoulder
like a clump of bird-manna
circuit sang out
he gloriously stretched
towards the anticlimax,
award ceremony for one
smiling into the microphone
of half-eaten cucumber
he clarified his position as knotted
muscle in the world's back,
tired string
of Penelope's sweater
he dimmed the kitchen lights
sat on the floor and spoke at length
with the growling whiteness
of the refrigerator.

GUIDED MEDITATION

All around you,
as far as the eye can see
nothing but soup.
Horizon, a broken zipper
of some deity's pants.
You're in a boat on loan
from the demon of Monday mornings.
Questions—birds—it's the fall
there're more of them
they form v's
traverse the sky towards
a shining yellow bottom
of a pot
where much better stuff
is being brewed.

HA-HA GALLERY

spinning like a sister   we've shot thru with pellets
a carnival's worth of time
over & over
in the ha-ha gallery

Steve Dalachinsky, *"blue #1"*

ha-ha gallery: seven grey shirts of history
untouchable behind the glass, patched—
one with the other, transfusion
of cotton skin,
continuity into sectarian nothingness, etc.
Now looking for seven oversized humans
willing to *shvitz* into our *objets d'art*,
add layers, complicate the bouquet—
also, looking for a typist
with nice calves and deliberately
imperfect pedicure, to typify
potential clientele, which is about to arrive any minute
or so we heard, though maybe misheard, that's our gallery for you, we sit and hear stuff
big big ears and everything yelling at the same time,
it's a ticklish chorus, world going everywhere at once,
did you know? one day all hyperlinks will point to a big nothing,
masked with blueness—everyone will click and fall, see you there
you'll be a desolate shade moving within desolation—
but we and our oversized humans will be wearing the shirts
you'll see us
art's gotta be utilitarian, even after the apocalypse,
the way architecture is today—
upward glass mushrooming on Bowery, good stuff, good art
is dead art, or so we heard, we hear lots of things, a ticklish chorus—remember?—
sign up for membership, our emails will arrive at yr door with the odor
of the abyss, the one laying between

our inboxes, we don't have location
or hours, we're not into time—or space, or visitors for that matter,
you're the first and last—it will all be smoke after you
how dreadful—so much work and—that's the joke, really,
yeah, ha-ha gallery, get it—
we even named this place after you

AUDIENCE PARTICIPATION
At Cecil Taylor concert, NYC, 08/31/09

dead on the snare, both sticks—
just laying there
the drummer bows
into his kit, into the direction of the music
picks the sticks up again
puts them down, silent, the bassist
opens eyes and mouth first time
this whole set the rhythm
section is sitting out—
four tense no-rhythm section minutes
perforated no-rhythm minutes
we were equals then, equally out
I equally with them also
ready to rush back in
yes! myriads of responses—
every move a riff:
focused affixing of the glasses:
zooming cosmic trombone!
tightened left buttock: eternal seal of approval!
bite into the finger: young cannibal
in love eating through
time, perforated time, sitting out time,
mapless, hatless, sitting out
I learned to breathe in the vacuum
look, look the bassist is drawing
with his bow, hieroglyphics in the dust—existential dust?
no, the plain grey floor kind . . .

WINTER SKETCH

mood ripples
like a puddle
      with a building inside
windows popping
widening
moving blotches of curtains
torso half-way
out, a man straps on a song
of a pinched nerve
fingers spread wide
they have no concept of holding—
only pointing towards
empty wires—
      blank lines across the note-sheet
that birds land on
in huddled phrases

EXCHANGE

At Marc Ribot Concert, The Stone, 11/2010

he heard someone talk
and wondered why the outside still
matters blowing
wordy breath on the shivering membrane
(their desire for hypnosis)
and there it was—he caught himself
talking in the middle of his own solo, retuning,
bunch of years went by
and folded into a pizzicato pocket
words were exchanged
at a surprisingly favorable rate
surprising for a row of tourists
circling his ruffled autobiography
bopping like Adam's apple
up and down his guitar neck

DEMI-TUBA

the world is falling out his pockets—
his pockets, deep as Sheol—
half-Zeus, half-worm expiring
pieces of sky, old wrappers—
if there's enough rain and cold
his pant will solidify into a tuba
a few holes and he's ready to blow
tender leg hair inside every note

KLEZMER BULLDOG

klezmer bulldog: with accordion
folds on his face
somewhere
in these folds there must be
a smile—a bulldog smile.
Bulldog, loyal servant of the human
misery
angry clown on strike he
won't wear a doggy coat! Or wash his feet! Shit into your bag!
Klezmer bulldog: wobbling is flirtatious
drool affectionate,
this is *not* about good looks baby or
some nebulous Gregorian nimbus chant
he'll growl into your tuba, come on
take out the goddamn tuba and let him growl into it!
He's gone beyond skepticism, sarcasm, beyond—
into intestinal neo-realism, gritty
but personable
it's really in now
Klezmer bulldog: imagine him on the cover of *Tikkun Magazine*
He gone sledding in Caucuses
saved babies in the Urals
hoisted his klezmer flag atop of the Carpathian mountains
all of his friends have sad, drooping clarinet noses
but he's got a pug, a button, cause his gramma mighta
been raped by a Mongolian Cossack Frenchman Henchman and
he won't let you forget that, no! he won't let you forget!

ROOTS

maybe because the urge to illuminate
was so strong, Naftule Branwein
liked to play his clarinet
wrapped in Christmas lights
and one time (true story)
somewhere in the Catskills
he *shvitzed* so much he electrocuted
his armpits and had to be carried off stage
like a deposed royalty
that he surely was
king of klezmer
but also grandson of the distinguished
Rabbi Yehuda Brandwein of Stretyn
true Chassidic blueblood
though admittedly not as popular as Shneur Zalman of Liadi,
the austere accountant of abstractions and ancestor of my own wife—
or Rabbi Noam Elimelech, heavy mystic from Lizhensk,
whose great-great-grandson Jeremy works at St. Marks bookstore, plays crazy altosax bebop
with some very famous people like Daniel Carter and David Krakauer
and me
we met at a klezmer punk show on the edges of still Chassidic Williamsburg where he was
standing at the bar reading Sun Ra's biography
back then we both had dandelion-style haircuts which you Americans call jewfro, but I like
dandelion better, and better yet,
oduvanchik in Russian.

MULBERRIES

After we came back from a year-long stay in Israel
it rained in New York almost daily for a month straight, a nice change from the desert
job market collapsed
I sat, purposeless, in front of the wet window for hours, and one morning,
walked down Bennett Ave, with a mug, picked mulberries
to present to my sweet wife, a feeble attempt at family providership from a stay-home dad, then
still childless, still crackling with memories of the branch I once sat on,
the mulberry tree across from my grandmother's house—
picking but not eating, trying to bring as much as possible home, for my parents,
to our then bare apartment on the seventh floor with no elevator,
the first co-op building in the town of Kirovograd.

June 24th, 2009

LOWER EAST SIDE OUTING

I help take the carriage down the steps while
baby's grandfather, the caretaker, locks cemetery gate
she's sleeping draped in cellophane
if anything she's too warm in there
says the grandmother smiling from behind her scarf
taking the last glance at the Jewish tombs dug
over three hundred years ago, we say our goodbyes
walk a block over where a free jazzer duo doesn't mind sounding smooth
or even pretty in an old synagogue restored for nostalgia's flowering lamps
there's even a little bell resounding at the end of the tune
I walk in on and look, another baby—squealing along with clarinet,
she shakes her little fist:
to hell with the whole concept of rhythm!
and silent grey and bald heads of the audience
are shaking a little too, maybe not for the same reason
maybe thinking: when did music become so distant
and we're always on the wrong side of the stage
in the meantime pianist forgot his glasses
and so he squints and leans over the synth,
sticks his nose right into the notes
poking and blurring the changes
and between songs he has a few things to say
about how we here on the Lower East Side no longer
communist enough and what about the stupidity of the warring world,
our album he says is called Voices in the Desert, it's on Zorn's label, he's got
a white bar-mitzvah yarmulkah and the clarinetist—a hip clown hat
he probably wears every day anyhow
the shul is on the border of Chinatown, and
the two babies will grow up into beautiful Nu Yorker mamas

TEL AVIV VIGNETTE

for Ruth Calderon

Tel Aviv shore café:
chairs line the evening beach
like rows in the synagogue
but, red and purple—
two bronze teenage gods
       male and female
fix up the lights
and dim them;
menus are stacked—
the gates? there are no gates!
Tonight, may the sea-worshipers
be as numerous as the grains of sand

NEGATIVE SPACE

what's changed
is nothing
nothing has changed
the nothing—the Big Nothing
has been altered! wow!
nothing's been shaken
from its blank slumber
nothing is alive
and walking—jay-walking!—through Brooklyn
inhaling the peanuts of lower Manhattan
nothing's the same now (meaning, it's not)
it changed, nothing as we know it
I believe! I believe we can change
nothing—the Great Nothing!

SOMETHING ABOUT REGGAE

dybbuk dozing in a creaking
summer chair
turned towards sunset creaking
on the edge of sleep
forgot his non-corporeal status
and for a minute thought he was
flesh again—melting in the summer bliss
and just then had a very human desire
to leave his body
and on the creaking
edge of sleep this seemed entirely logical
as did the djembe trek behind his left ear
and someone's baritone harmonizing with—
nothing? sunset itself?
and the tender golden sun red at the bottom
set behind the green shrubs like a Rastafarian flag
spread across the horizon
I will leave my body he wailed
that's it! that, it's that, it is it's
quacking duck-dubs echoed all around
limbs spread wide, he leaped out of the chair
only to find he's got no feet to land on,
no hips to sway, no belly to pull him down—
and so continued floating on a memory raft
of a summer-time reggae dream

EAR TO THE GOURD

On Elliott Sharp's interpretations of Monk

what I hear
is my stomach
what I hear
is the stone-lit sadness
dog of a memory
chewing the leash
a glob of future
in these here lungs
wet socks
monkfish monk*fish*
turn everything we know into a turn
hyphens as answers,
stitching the ripping self and
       psychosis as chops
a cover from across
the ocean is dis-cover, all I want
is you with, ear nailed to yr doorpost—back
door of self-reinvention where we meet,

                             dear Ruby.

Skin Orchestra

for J.C. Jones

dust blows through the saxophone

scribal dust, grey self-addressed letters,
voices of Adam's dusted dream of all of us
dream of dust that became skin—

cold skin—cold under the stars—inside a black book-flap—night-sky of early saxophone text—

skin sings out   u think this is music? do you think this constant sensation of loss gradation of
loss puffed cheeks of upset this is music? obsessive riffs on the leash   political sprinkling of
saliva on the friend's jacket   soul of garlic   rolodex of cravings who is singing   this system
held by the system breath by breath door by door disease of building hammering—music?—
obsessive staccato!   I've been attached, plastered on like foster care   is it for my sake that the
sun comes out is it for my sake that soup cans are sealed—in Brooklyn?! for my secrets? I'd rather

practical mind: practical as a refrigerator
practical mind: prolific and well-modulated

there're greater pleasures—
like sinking into the self unearthing the violence with hungry eyes, knowing this is not me this is
only where I found me in this machinery   sad construction of bone and musical skin   conductor
the lone chopstick over the abyss how far down

Neanderthals scratch
themselves absentmindedly
a savage scratching in the cold
maybe next to another one maybe
next to another two maybes
a tribe of maybes
sky full of maybe sky full of non-committal noon-pain-joy sky full of sun above snow and very
scratchy skin   a lot fewer teeth than necessary   hunger and other demoralizing factors

great sage savage scratch session   behind the ear tip of the nose barbaric thighs music of granting impulse—to get out of yrself—shed the skin—shed the body—over the cliff—gone— black paint over canvas—

and in the gone space, free of backbones and music in the heavy nothing there hangs a sleepy carpet of a word—all one big letter? one big chain of letters? a chain we're chained with? or is it all . . . is it all?

BASS SOLO

begun roughly denouncing
the old method: juicy, all-too middle-
Eastern dance of thighs and turkey
drumsticks, he plucked
feathers out of *that* hat, pressed all
air outta that self-copy
like a body to-be-left-behind
a rug to stomp on
and the others? didn't misunderstand—
but floated in on their own time zones,
sky time-signatures / packed boogie-clouds
—on the edges of his painting of self-rejection

but then he got very forgiving, lightly pullling
remaining petals and bodypaarts
and the word-stringgs and before longg
everyone knew this wasn't really about remorse or self-empathy
but pleasuring—better—as after a fight,
probably pleasuring
the self
and isn't it always?
always a memory on top of a memory—if in real time—
or on borrowed—

or to be more pre-cise it's the
burrowing
into the quarter-tone, penetrating it, really knowing how:
nose first
and others said: why not, makes for an easier birth like this
if only he didn't have that whole "out" thing rehearsed for generations, y'know—
forced out, cut out, left out,
how's that for a metaphor of understanding cosmos?
left-out-way-out-out-west-out-yes-west, west of orgasm, south-west—

i.e., definitely in the right direction, not there quite yet
but sooon maybe, and this sati-

sfaction ssettled in, yess, ssooon, it'ss
the woodss we'vve all been to
beef-ore & didn't no-tease how he got there & didn't expect
we'd get this far in so quickly, see—no need
for those over-spiced thighs, more tango

is what this world needs, clearly
tango under a red blanket
of loneliness, uniquely Jewish,
                                        (a phrase he learned from his wife this evening)
that's right loneliness, uniquely Jewish—
our long cramped aristocracy—
so this is what he's been talking about this whole time!
not so surprising that his intestinal Jewish balloon filled up and
lifted him out of the forest of all of you

but then what does he know about it, really—
                        in his beige assimilated pants, maybe
it's the whole world's beige or even if not, these words anyhow
were put into his mouth by a bearded
photograph, or a million
of them, all he is   gigantic collage of bearded photographs,
from last century-and-a-half, archive of their inton'AYshions,

and others? Could relate, also photographs in their essence,
so it was a room of snap-shots
archival polaroid body-parts, giving off scent in unison
            and their bouquet

                is for you

blessings
and flossings of the blessings from between your green well-meaning teeth

thaaaaaaat's what this is about—a certain shaky still-life of beard, bouquet & your snapping teeth

at first sight unsympathetic, but then wait, is that a smile—or just
our dried out skulls,

      happy to see each other?

at Deep Tones for Peace
April 26-27, 2009

THE BASS: INITIATION

Ella was a bassist and did not know it. The way she found out was like this. "Like this, and like that," the radio was going off, as she stood behind the counter of the Esperanto Café, laying whip cream *thick* over a cup of hot cider. Change ringing in the slammed register. Crackling noise of piped heat, her co-worker wiping the cappuccino whipper with a gentle towel, holding on to the protruding machinery a second too long. The music. Entrance door wheezes. Then the bathroom door. Entrance door wheezes, huffing delivery man drops the package—pipes sing, register slams, change dangles. Co-worker mixes another cappuccino—shoowhooshawashoo—hiiiigh pitch voice rises from a table in the left corner, someone's hand goes up "check please"— "excuse me my tea…"—"fuck them and their oil"—delivery man and his boxes, and the boxes' boxes tumble downstairs. Register. Hiiiigh. Register. There is a needle, threading it all, a hungry needle pulling everything together—slam—like Joseph's coat. "... waited for her, freezing like she was some kinda of a Messiah"—this last one was actually not anything anyone in the café said, it was someone's thought, not Ella's own, she was sure, and it was no telepathy either, though maybe telepathy's psychotic cousin, nameless cousin—door wheezes—"Grandma, let me be completely honest with you . . . "—cousin nameless but known in jazz sweat, in concentration-plucked jazz lips, corner of a yes, suddenly unfolded table with enough room for everyone, with enough room, enough, . . . oughfff, ufff, she didn't know it, didn't know she was a bassist for another half-minute. Till the man, whose thought she might have heard, or who maybe heard the same thought she did, or maybe heard something completely different, but *heard* it, with heard hearing, with shearing uh shredding fingers that he dangled over the table as if playing a slanted piano, or typing on a rock, or stretching the stiff fingers in the warmth of Esperanto, with its slam! and cappuccino shoowhooshawashoo, across the noise, like an octopus, fingers out, as she brought his wwhipped cider to him, the second the cup sat down, her head was grooving a little like this and like that, as his fingers landed on the table beside the cup, around the cup, kept playing the surfaces, percussive, silent across the noise, foot pressing the leg of the table like an invisible pedal riding them out of the hiiiigh and register, past this winter, and cider, which they both understood, was not cider, but *seder*—the order, universal order-*seder* of the needle that sows Joseph's coat, out of shreds of the microcosmic café reality, and he knew she was a bassist, and she did too—even before he said—"Everything is a bass you know, you will lose it trying to play, or grow very, very large" and she retorted: "Bass is Nothing, a black lamp, but when you hit the string against the fret, blindness becomes hope, which then splinters and dies and then it's time to look for another note, I think, though I don't believe we're in disagreement."

WINTER HAIKU

first cold winter night
blinking and growling under the table
modem and router

WORK LIFE

office is this
enthusiastic greeting and then a drop
eyes sliding down the elevator buttons
we simply have nothing
to say and hate the still-
lingering need to.
A few of us brush teeth after lunch.
Small, but dedicated contingent.
All day I drag and paste and
make sure the numbers add up
across & diagonally. Well-meaning boss
tells me I need more confidence—
speaks jovially, with office
door open so all can hear.
Gogol and Kafka knew it both:
smallness of a nut in the machinery
that does things you don't want to think about.
Then you begin to think of the universe
the same way.

2010

To the Man Who Saw Me Giving Thumbs Up to the Office Urinal

Overheard Poem

it didn't work the first time around
or second
but gave in on the third
I wanted to show my approval
I'm impulsive about positive reinforcement
but in the process of doing this
I noticed your back shuffling past me
I thought I'd explain myself
but you were already behind the closed door of the stall
and I figured that addressing you there
on this matter
might only exacerbate the situation

FOOTPRINTS

In the dim bathroom light
ego eyes stare into the tripartite mirror
the lamp's bottom made of colored glass
cup of mints, wicker basket with paper-towels
thought moves uncaffeinated, slow winter
fly, and the plunger
speckled with paint
café voices crowd behind the locked door
"things I have to give to the world"
the trashcan is retro, brass-like, plastic,
through the crack in the window,
three day old snow
that's been stomped on by thousands.

ESCALATOR

Opening his eyes Y found himself at the foot of the escalator at standstill. It was empty, though not entirely: the way some public sites are so overcrowded during the day that even in the after-hours they retain a certain weight, shadowy dent in the pool of vacated space. On top of the escalator stood a folding plastic chair. Whoever it was meant for did not leave the impression of his form on it though, leading one to think it may never have been designated for anyone specific, but a carnivalesque go-around of bodies in need of rest or self-assertion as a body in the midst of this—this?

What raced through Y's mind—instead of his whereabouts—was a vintage memory of waking up in his cousin's room, on the third night of the visit, completely disoriented by positioning of his cot, layout of the room, and then, following the recognition, certain nostalgic wish to be back inside the confusion of half-second ago, the between/both space, to look at the darkness straining to recognize shapes within it.

Whatever has landed Y in this position, in this place, was probably not a good thing. Nevertheless, there was no pain, and breathing remained steady. His thoughts were quiet, certainly there, but as if somewhat muted, volume turned to 2 instead of the usual 6. He couldn't remember the details: last thing that happened, his name / age / what he looked like in the mirror, yet he knew himself, was ok with that alone, the mere familiar cadence of his thoughts. Even this sensation of being "once-removed" did not feel altogether foreign.

The panic—also, unmistakably his—lingered somewhere at a distance, static, like a house seen from a mountaintop, hazy roof across miles of summer heat. "I can get up if I want to" he thought, "or rather: I know myself as someone who could."

In his early teens, it often happened that he'd fall asleep and then, somewhere halfway in, he half-found himself, struggled to either wake up or fall back asleep, inevitably getting too worked up for the latter, just wanting to wake up and give this another try, but could not rip himself through the net-like layer over him, which was terrifying at the time, and would have been now, except what Y was experiencing at the moment was a bit different.

Then everything came back.

Subway map badly folded in his pocket pushed into his crotch. Aftertaste of the swirling shoes that stepped on his eyes, stilettos burrowing into his temples, flip-flops that slapped his ears.

He must have found a nook, away from it all, passed out, and unconscious dragged himself back here, to the foot of the escalator, after the store's closing.

It's miraculous no alarm has sounded. Or maybe it did? He imagined re-telling the story many years down the road: "Not for me, this country, not for me." Or: "My son took his TOEFL, I went holiday shopping. We both failed and then woke up and recovered in a few years." And then: "We're made of something other than the people here, and something else other than the people there, we're bird-folks, blotchy-faced, meatless seekers, and it is only in the spirit of a random impulse we found ourselves across the ocean, the ultimate result of which, for me, was a shopping spree, rows of shoes I have struggled against, and will continue doing so, probably my whole life, or at least until I become someone else, a new name staring back from a new passport.

Will I then know to find my body? Recognize and tease myself out of another blank-out? Will there be another one? I know who I am. Airplane, birds, grandchildren, shoes." He suddenly understood that where he belonged was on the plastic folding chair on top of the escalator. He rose up. No alarm sounded.

ACCIDENT

I wasn't the only one in a crowd leisurely sitting around the Lincoln Center fountain, who turned for a double-dose of this tall, immaculately dressed man with blue plastic glasses, through which his eyes peered with frenzy comparable to those whose lives are brutally threatened. When we all heard the screech of tires, a honk that lasted three unbearably long seconds, we also saw, in slow motion, the man's neck jerking towards Columbus avenue, his body half-turning, half-falling in the direction of the screech. He shot a quick glance at the Avery Fisher Hall, raising his hand in half-wave, half-thrash, and another man, dressed more casually, rushed in his direction, as they merged in their race towards the screech. Two Chagalls hanging on the side of the Met like the building's gigantic breasts, were veiled with thick white curtains, probably to shield them from the heat, though red blotches of the left side of one them were visible, bleeding quiet grumpiness on the otherwise golden square, gilded by July sun. Moving so quickly within the fountain drops, the sun seemed to be the only truly living thing at the moment, while our minds and attention spans, our self-protective impulses melted like walls of long-besieged city. Tourists, uncomfortable as they always are with anything that isn't scripted in a guidebook, blabbered in various languages and dialects, while New Yorkers, trained to sniff out & dismiss a false alarm without raising the eyes from the smart-phones, this time around, knew this wasn't a fakeout. More than a few of us started towards the site of the accident. By the time I reached the steps leading down to Columbus, the two men turned their backs to the avenue and were strolling back, each holding a hand of a six-year-old girl, in a green printed dress, blond hair on her shoulders. All three, to different degrees, bore expressions of blankness: people with faces of answering machines too full for another message – even the little girl was blank and silent, shuffling quietly in her flip-flops, as the three of them angled, turning towards the gelato stand.

THE NARRATIVE

Something Faustian about my ticket to New York
laced with soul's awakening
to realities of my old-world great-grandparents;
there might be a farce or sermon in that
I think and grow irritated—
because I'm not
anyone's tale, least of all my own
and how colonizing to horde
life's ironies into one pen like that—
or am I now, bargaining?
For isn't myth but a buying
of time, renting room in the back
of the mask, for a private audience
with a few questions
I'm never going to want to answer?

September 2011

3

BACHELOR'S HAIKU

spring evening at home
folding up the warm laundry
  one unmatched sock

RACHMONOS BLUES

I know a little woman,
she got a truck full of rach-
monos, yeah a truck full of parsnips and rach-
monos   wonder if she'll park it on my street tonight

Rachmonos (Yiddish/Hebrew): Mercy.

MODERN DANCE

What's natural is
our helpless/infantile   awkwardness who says
dancing needs to be smooth or graceful what's
this a ballet? or the three cocktail internal samba blare hey man
don't look at my girl like that it's not
that she doesnt know how to dance, it's not that
she has no sense of rhythm
you just don't know what the dance is
        contorted self-wrestle-catharsis-pharisee-jean-rub-free-gene-stumble-stomp-epileptic
        futuristic & alien, VERY alien
you smooth you lose, lose my attention
I'm done laughing at yo beat-articulating back-pocket
melody punctured head-bop school uniform hack
me & my girl are espousing
new aesthetics for the rest of the universe
but don't watch us we'll get more self-conscious and split
split the dancefloor
        cause my name is Ornette Korach Coleman Picklejuice Pediatrician
and I'll heal you, bring some hairy Ashkenazi medicine on yo
smooth little *tuchas*.

Tuchas (Yiddish): a behind.

NOTE TO S—

Dear S—,

After you left and I returned to R—, you won't believe it, no—I won't believe it, no—no one who's ever believed (if for a second) with any sort of fervor, or verve, or even a simple, barbaric head-cracking eagerness—and that, I think covers the whole world, except for the dichotomous Janus-faced people of Zevulun who only believe in the purity of the late-night misanthropic moaning session (which is why they prefer to remain a lost tribe—moaning in the desert is dangerous since the hedgehogs go after anyone moaning—and unless you're into that—which Zevulun people were not—but they've had plenty of sensuous, tender moments with gerbils, that's a fact (and we hardly have any facts related to these renegade tribesmen, all we have is their national anthem which extensively references gerbils, and there was a solid cover-version of it made by, no less, Chava Alberstein, of whom, to be honest, I don't know nothing about, I just saw her name on your ipod and it sunk into my sink as, in fact, lots of you-related words have, whether from the ipod or the lip, or the cheek, or like that time on shabbos when I said somebody's-I-won't-specify-whose neurosis is size of the elephant and you said don't you dare put that in the poem, after which I decided I must)), and by the holy Holy!, I am certain that Baal Shem Tov was a little off when he said that a broken heart is the key to all rooms in the Master's chamber, it ain't no broken heart—everybody's heart is a broken heart since the womb out-outbreak, what's new, but no, dearest S—, it's all about the misanthropic moaning session, which subsumes broken hearts, and—twisted ankles, rattled nut-sacks, brutally scratched bald-spots—lots of things, and I'll confess, probably to my own detriment that I consider kvetching to be the refined, urbanized-after-shtetelized, more subtle version of moaning, and so sometimes when you kvetch, the door of the Master's chamber is wide open, and so is my bedroom door, and my kitchen door (which is a non-door—just a door-post—and its always open—but *kol vahomer* (*Heb*: all the more so)) and so even if I make fun of you for kvetching, I like you no less for it, to say the least, but don't take it into yo head, not the upper part of it anyway, the brain-basement is fine though, and also please take it into your lips, yes, please, yes, take my words, and your words, and your momma's (actually, nevermind on that) like they're over-ripe cherries, cherry
orchard import, wholly tangential, A.D.D. showdown, but what gentleness isn't tan-

gential, I mean, served straight-up its too sweet for a Brooklyn-peppered, Russian-Jew-style-pickled, woman in the full blossom of her eye-shadow-foreign-film-sexy-knees-sarcasm, and by holy Holy! that's way too sweet for me too, and so the only way, the only one way is the gently angular ever-elbowing tangent, that, yes, I mean what more, what more can I ever tell you?

FAMILY FORMATIONS

now i'm your mother
and you're mine
we're both newly crowned orphans
immediately repossessed
immediately childless, immediately siblings
equally lonely unaware shoulder blades glued to each other to de-wing
Orphic breasts of myth & blind infantile appetite for dreams and loss
we'll breastfeed each other with abandon
and dross, I'm your mother, you hear, the only one
in the orphanage of our house, under own
orphaned blanket, this blanket of many colors we're trunkless, leafless this cold winter,
we're a pack of maniac roots suspended three inches above the bed
root-snake-pit under the blanket, mouthfuls of each other
no soil to take from; no leaves to give to;
nothing but own nerve endings to sink teeth
in, I am your mother and you're mine
you're the moon-brothers and I'm the misty-eyed Egyptian ruler
I am the Midianite caravan of slave-drivers extending
your orphaned hands to our orphaned snake-face

KICKS

we got the word
from the womb
word is: kicks!
Shana calls me at work:
"I felt it, twice!"
and I go into my excited/
freaked out/free-associative literary zone
thinking Kerouac and his kicks
always with his kicks
anyway why is the baby kicking?
will grow up a soccer player—
like the great-uncle back in the old country?
"it's just moving like all
things living" says Shana
you hear? living! in its
expanding house of next
five months, I been
watching my wife's belly
rounding off like our own private
pocket moon
rising over the reverb of morning thrashings
and now—bang! boom! knock-knock!
who goes there?
give a look—*gib a kik*—
a kick! I get a kick
outta you!

SOUL SHAKEDOWN

Vacuum cleaner or a hair-blower
our doctor tells us
is what the womb sounds like
(from the inside)
so bring on the white noise
to soothe your infant.
The rabbis say in the womb
babies learn Talmud
with all the commentaries but
forget it on the way out
that's why they cry so much—
bring on the honeyed Talmud nostalgia
to soothe your infant.
But the way our 2 month old
goes from apocalyptic bawling
to happy smiles when
I put Bob Marley and the Wailers on
I think maybe
while studying Talmud
with angelic Vacuum Cleaner he was also
bopping in his private soul shakedown
party dream, heart thumping liquefied bass
rhythm guitar chirping like spirit's matchstick
at the spinning wheel of eternity.

FAMILY STILL LIFE

In solidarity, my bike
hasn't touched the street
since the pregnancy
the angel of wheels
stands nostalgically in the hallway—
sometimes, my mother-in-law,
when she comes over
and changes to relax,
hangs her wig
on its handlebars.

February 2011

Post-Face

I was born in a provincial town in the Ukrainian steppes, halfway between Kiev and Odessa. In 1995, at the age of fifteen–the week of Jerry Garcia's passing–I came to the United States. I arrived as an exchange student, without much English or plans, but liked it and stayed. Still not entirely certain what prompted my interest in traditional Judaism (of which I knew nothing growing up), but the pull was intense and irrational. As such things ought to be, I think. Consequently, I attended Yeshiva University in New York. I became involved with *Mima'amakim Journal of Jewish Art*, which, for a number of years, I edited. In the years following, I discovered New York's performance poetry world as well as the world of free jazz, both fluid arts that live above the typed-up pages and note-sheets. I also began my Ph.D. at the Comp Lit department of the CUNY Graduate Center, and started writing poetry and music reviews for the *Forward*. In 2008, having just married, my wife Shoshana and I traveled to Jerusalem, where, for a year, I was a Dorot Fellow. It was during that time that the idea of using Talmudic rhetoric and jazz rhythm/mythology on the shared dialectic grounds came about.

The poems collected in this volume are also part of the evolving jazz-poetry performance project, which premiered in September 2010 at the Cell Theater in New York, featuring the 15-piece Ayn Sof Arkestra under the direction of Frank London and Greg Wall. In January 2011, the project expanded to include a notable hermeneuticist and a great muse, my son Lev Zalman.

I should also add that during the day I work at Random House Publishing and that facts of one's biography have little, if anything, to do with one's biography.

ACKNOWLEDGEMENTS

First and foremost, I'd like to thank my publisher and editor, poet-sage Stanley Moss. Also, big thanks to his amazing team—Reiko Davis and Adrienne Davich at The Sheep Meadow Press.

Much gratitude to the Dorot Foundation for providing the space and time in which a number of these poems were conceived. Special thanks to the Dorot Fellowship's director Steve Jacobson for all of his continued support and encouragement.

Deep gratitude to people whose music and/or words and friendship blew my mind and informed various poems in this collection: JC Jones, Steve Dalachinsky, Rabbi Greg Wall, Frank London, Avivah Zornberg, Matthue "Jupiter" Roth, Will Lee, Sipai Klein, Adam Shechter, and Eve Grubin.

Big warm mishpoche gratitude to the Shinefields and the Olidorts.

As always, I'm grateful to my parents, my aunt, and my grandparents—on both sides of the Divide.

And of course, at all times, I'm endlessly thankful to/for Shana and Lev, to whom this book is dedicated.